SCRUMPTIOUS HOME BAKING

50 favourite recipes to make and share

www.diverseabilitiesplus.org.uk

THANK YOU

Special thanks goes to White Pepper, for all the support, advice and direction given to Diverse Abilities Plus. White Pepper very generously loaned Diverse Abilities Plus their fully equipped cookery school kitchen to produce all the cakes and puddings ready to be photographed for this book.

www.white-pepper.co.uk

Sincere thanks also to Steve Cook of **www.seeker.uk.com** for giving up his time to do the great photography for the book.

A big thank you to our baking team who donated their time for two mammoth days of non-stop baking:
Samantha Randle – **www.corfecakesandbakes.co.uk**
Coral Turan – **www.cupcakesbournemouth.co.uk**
Luke Stuart – **www.white-pepper.co.uk**
Sandra Blainey
Michelle Connor
Sadie Smith

For the use of their premises and equipment on our baking days we would like to thank:
Bergere Interiors – **www.bergereinteriors.co.uk**
The Rural Farm Shop Company – **www.theruralfarmshopcompany.com**
The Dorset Charcuterie Company

Many thanks to Basepoint in Bournemouth who will make a donation to Diverse Abilities Plus in line with the sales of this book. **www.basepoint.co.uk**

Thanks also to those who donated prizes for our recipe competition, including White Pepper Cookery School, Coral Turan of Rex's Heavenly Cupcakes and Julia's Kitchen (**www.therealfoodcookeryschool.co.uk**).

We would like to thank everyone who took the time to submit their favourite recipes for this cookbook.

BASEPOINT
making a difference

Seeker
.uk.com

WHITE PEPPER

HELLO

Life can seem so hectic and stressful, finding quality time to spend with our families is difficult and for our family it is made even more difficult as our oldest son James has profound disabilities. Finding an activity that we can all enjoy is not easy, the one activity that brings us together as a family is baking.

I have a passion for baking. I began baking at a very young age with my mum and I now bake with my children, and my children still bake with their Granny. I truly believe that anyone can enjoy the experience of baking regardless of disability, it is one of the few activities that stimulates all of your senses, James' disability makes it difficult to physically participate but he gets so much sensory stimulation in other ways; the gorgeous aromas, the array of sounds from mixers, the taste and of course seeing the end result.

This book contains recipes for all to enjoy, from the most basic of recipes to recipes for those of you who like a bit of a challenge. Recipes were collected for this book through a competition run by Diverse Abilities Plus; each recipe is either a favourite recipe or has a special memory or little story behind it.

The making of this book has bought so many people together from within the charity and the local community with entries coming from the children, young people and adults that are supported by Diverse Abilities Plus, staff, families, siblings, volunteers, local businesses, esteemed local chefs and celebrities.

Through buying this book you are helping Diverse Abilities Plus to continue its great work through services and projects for children and adults with physical and learning disabilities. Words cannot express what a positive effect the charity has on the lives of the people supported.

Your support will help the charity make a huge difference for children, young people and adults with disabilities.

Happy Baking

Sadie Smith

CONTENTS

"Delicious cakes, muffins and cupcakes for tea or not for tea!"

Afternoon tea

BAILEYS CUPCAKES

"These are great cakes for fundraising; I add a sugar butterfly and use them as Langside School cakes as the butterfly is their emblem."

SUBMITTED BY NICOLA ROPER, WHOSE DAUGTHER ATTENDS LANGSIDE SCHOOL

- 350g margarine
- 350g granulated sugar
- 6 eggs
- 350g self raising flour
- 4 tablespoons of Baileys liqueur

Icing:
- 225g butter
- 450g icing sugar
- 2 tablespoons of Baileys liqueur

Decoration of choice or to make sugar butterflies:
- 1 egg white
- 300g icing sugar
- 2 teaspoons gum tragacanth
- Colouring of choice

TOP TIP

To simplify this recipe, instead of making butterflies you can choose any decoration for the top. It looks very good with milk chocolate curls placed on top of the icing swirl.

1. Preheat the oven to 160°C/gas 3.

2. Cream the margarine and sugar until light and fluffy.

3. Gradually beat in the eggs a little at a time.

4. Add the Baileys liqueur, one spoon at a time and mix well.

5. Fold in flour until fully incorporated.

6. Spoon into 24 cup cases and cook for 25 minutes.

7. Cool on a wire rack.

8. To make the icing, cream together the icing sugar and butter.

9. Add Baileys liqueur and mix well.

10. Pipe a swirl onto the top of each cake.

11. To make the sugar butterflies, mix all the ingredients together, adding a few drops of your desired colour.

12. Knead well, roll and cut out butterflies.

13. Dry on a folded piece of paper to get the butterfly flying shape.

14. Paint as required, using edible paints and glitter.

CARROT CAKE

"This is a great recipe. My children used to love to help me make it. Now they make it with their children."

- 175g light muscovado sugar
- 175ml sunflower oil
- 4 medium eggs
- 4 medium sized carrots
- 110g raisins
- Grated zest of 1 orange
- 175g self raising flour

- 1 teaspoon bicarbonate of soda
- 1 teaspoon ground cinnamon
- ½ teaspoon nutmeg

Icing:

- 175g icing sugar
- 2 tablespoons orange juice

SUBMITTED BY ROS BLISHEN. MEMBER OF THE FUNDRAISING TEAM AT DIVERSE ABILITIES PLUS

1. Preheat the oven to 180°C/gas 4.

2. Peel, wash and grate the carrots.

3. Grease and line the base and sides of an 18cm square cake tin.

4. Put the sugar into a large mixing bowl, pour in the oil then add the beaten eggs, mix well with a wooden spoon.

5. Stir in the carrots, raisins and orange rind.

6. Mix the flour, bicarbonate of soda and spices, then sift into the bowl. Mix ingredients thoroughly.

7. Pour into the prepared tin, the mixture will be quite runny.

8. Cook for 40 – 45 minutes, until it feels firm and springy when you press the centre with your fingertip.

9. Cool in the tin for a few minutes then turn it onto a wire cooling rack.

10. Beat together the icing sugar and orange juice until smooth, drizzle over the carrot cake, letting it drip down the sides.

CHOCOLATE & STRAWBERRY MARBLE CUPCAKES

SUBMITTED BY CORAL TURAN FROM REX'S HEAVENLY CUPCAKES

"I love this marble cupcake recipe as it combines chocolate and strawberry in one and looks fantastic with the two different sponges mixed together. I am very pleased to be supporting Diverse Abilities Plus as the money raised from this cookery book will help them continue to give their much needed work."

- 175g margarine
- 175g self raising flour
- 175g caster sugar
- 3 large eggs, beaten
- 1 teaspoon baking powder
- 1 teaspoon strawberry flavouring
- ½ tablespoon of cocoa powder
- Pink food colouring

Topping:
- 500g icing sugar
- 110g unsalted butter
- 60ml semi skimmed milk
- Pink food colouring

1. Preheat the oven to 160°C/gas 3.

2. Line a 12 hole muffin tin with paper cake cases.

3. Beat together the butter and sugar in a large bowl until light and creamy.

4. Add 3 beaten eggs and beat well.

5. Sift the flour and baking powder into the mixture and stir well.

6. Divide the mixture into two bowls. In the first add the cocoa powder and mix well, in the other add one teaspoon of pink colouring and ½ teaspoon of strawberry flavouring, mix well.

7. Spoon alternate chocolate and strawberry mixture into the cases until the case is two thirds full.

8. Then run a knife through the mixture to make a marble effect in the sponge.

9. Cook for 20 minutes, and then allow to cool on a wire rack.

10. To decorate the cupcakes, mix the icing sugar, butter, and ½ teaspoon of strawberry flavouring, milk and a little pink food colouring. Beat until smooth.

11. Using a large nozzle, swirl the icing on the top of the cupcakes.

12. Add decoration.

FRUIT SCONES

"No afternoon tea is complete without scones."

- 250g self raising flour
- 50g caster sugar
- 50g butter, chilled and diced
- 1 egg

- 100ml milk
- 50g sultanas or other dried fruit

1. Preheat the oven to 220°C/gas 7.

2. Sift the flour into a bowl and mix in sugar.

3. Add the butter and rub into the flour using the tips of your fingers, until the mixture resembles fine bread crumbs.

4. Stir in the sultanas.

5. Beat the egg with the milk.

6. Make a well in the centre of the dry ingredients and pour in the egg mixture a little at a time bringing the mixture together with your hands to form a dough.

7. Roll out dough until about 3cm thick. Using a pastry cutter, stamp out a circle of dough and place on a warm baking tray.

8. Cook for 10 – 12 minutes until golden brown, transfer to a wire cooling rack.

SUBMITTED BY RITA BRIGHT, WHOSE GRANDSON ATTENDS LANGSIDE SCHOOL, SMITHERS & PROJECT MY TIME

TOP TIP

Eat on the day of baking, especially whilst warm with a good quality strawberry jam and a generous spoonful of clotted cream.

ISOBEL'S MOCHA SLICES

A recipe given to me by my good friend Isobel. It reminds me of our group of friends who met whilst doing an outdoor exercise class with our babies. Those babies are now all at school but we still regularly meet up for a cuppa, slice of cake and a good old natter."

SUBMITTED BY SADIE SMITH, A PARENT WHOSE CHILD IS SUPPORTED BY SEVERAL DIVERSE ABILITIES PLUS SERVICES

- 225g margarine
- 225g granulated sugar
- 225g self raising flour
- 150g oats
- 50g cocoa powder

Topping:
- 50g margarine
- 1 dessertspoon of coffee granules dissolved in a little boiling water
- 225g icing sugar

1. Preheat the oven to 180°C/gas 4.

2. Melt the margarine in a saucepan.

3. Stir in the sugar, flour, oats and cocoa powder.

4. Press into a rectangular greased tin.

5. Cook for 15 minutes, no longer than this as it will go too hard.

6. To make the topping, melt the margarine in a saucepan.

7. Add the dissolved coffee and mix well.

8. Take the pan off the heat and beat in the icing sugar until all the lumps have disappeared.

9. Spread over the base, when set cut into squares.

LISA'S LIPSMACKING LEMON CURD CUPCAKES

Submitted by Lisa Reardon whose husband is a committed volunteer for Diverse Abilities Plus

"Lisa's husband Paul joined Diverse Abilities Plus as a Trustee three years ago. Although he is no longer a Trustee he still volunteers at Barnabas, the charity's adult day opportunities project, three days a week."

- 175g self raising flour
- 1 teaspoon baking powder
- 175g butter (at room temperature)
- 175g caster sugar
- 3 eggs
- Grated rind of 1 lemon
- 1 tablespoon lemon juice

Lemon curd:
- 75g caster sugar
- Grated rind & juice of 1 lemon
- 2 eggs
- 50g unsalted butter

Icing:
- 300g icing sugar
- 125g butter
- Zest of 1 lemon
- 2-3 teaspoons lemon juice

1. Preheat oven to 170°C/gas 3.

2. Fill a 12 cup muffin tray with paper cases.

3. Put all the cake ingredients into a bowl and whisk until smooth.

4. Divide into the paper cases and cook for approx 25 minutes or until golden brown.

5. To make the lemon curd, place the caster sugar and grated rind in a bowl.

6. In a separate bowl, whisk the lemon juice and eggs, and then pour this over the sugar and rind.

7. Cut butter into small chunks and add to the bowl.

8. Place the bowl over a pan of simmering water and stir until it has thickened.

9. When the cakes are cold, scoop out some of the sponge from the middle and replace with a teaspoon of the lemon curd.

10. To make the butter icing, beat together the icing sugar and butter until pale and fluffy, add the lemon zest and juice and beat for a little while longer.

11. Spread or pipe a swirl of icing on the top of each cake.

12. To decorate either scatter with lemon zest or top with yellow sugar flowers.

RED VELVET CAKE

"I love this recipe; it's the most curious of all the cakes I've ever come across."

- 120g unsalted butter, softened
- 300g caster sugar
- 2 large eggs
- 20g cocoa powder
- 40ml red food colouring
- 1 teaspoon vanilla essence
- 300g self raising flour
- 1 teaspoon salt
- 150ml semi skimmed milk

- 90g plain yogurt
- 3 teaspoons white wine vinegar
- 1 teaspoon bicarbonate of soda

Frosting:

- 100g unsalted butter
- 600g icing sugar
- 250g full fat soft cheese
- Sprinkles or decoration of your choice

SUBMITTED BY SAMANTHA RANDLE, CORFE CAKES AND BAKES

1. Preheat the oven to 190°C/gas 5.

2. Grease and line three 8" sandwich tins.

3. Cream together the butter and sugar until pale and fluffy.

4. Beat the eggs and add a little at a time, beating thoroughly after each addition.

5. In a separate bowl, stir together the cocoa powder, food colouring and vanilla essence to form a paste.

6. Add the paste to the batter mixture, mixing thoroughly until the paste is completely incorporated.

7. Sift the flour and salt into a separate bowl.

8. In a jug mix together the milk and yogurt.

9. Add the flour to the batter in two batches, alternating with the milk and yogurt. Beat well after each addition.

10. In a bowl mix together the vinegar and bicarbonate of soda, then add to the cake mixture. Stir well.

11. Divide the mixture between the tins and cook for 20 – 25 minutes until the top feels springy when pressed with fingertips.

12. Allow the cakes to cool for a while in the tin, and then turn out onto a wire rack.

13. For the frosting, beat the butter and icing sugar together until the mixture is a sandy texture.

14. Add the cream cheese and mix together until everything is incorporated, continue to beat until the frosting is soft and fluffy.

15. To decorate, spread frosting between each slice, placing layers on top of each other. Once assembled spread frosting over the sides and top.

16. Finish as desired.

ROSE & RASPBERRY LITTLE CREAM SPONGES

"These cakes look almost too good to eat."

- 175g unsalted butter
- 175g caster sugar
- 3 large eggs, beaten
- 150g self raising flour
- 25g cornflour
- 1 teaspoon baking powder
- 2 tablespoons of rosewater

Filling:
- 300ml double cream
- 2 tablespoons of rosewater
- Raspberry jam

Topping:
- Sifted icing sugar
- Fresh raspberries

RECIPE SUBMITTED BY JULIA'S KITCHEN

1. Preheat the oven to 160°C/gas 3.
2. Grease a 12 hole muffin tin with a little butter.
3. Beat together the butter and sugar until pale and fluffy.
4. Gradually beat in the eggs.
5. Sift in the flours and baking powder, gently folding into the mixture until it is fully incorporated.
6. Divide the mixture into the muffin tray.
7. Cook for about 20 minutes, cool the cakes on a wire rack.
8. Whip the cream until it forms soft peaks.
9. When the cakes are cool, cut in half and spread one half with jam and cream, top with second half.
10. Top with berries and dust with sifted icing sugar.

SUMMER BERRY MUFFINS

"This recipe reminds me of all the lovely fruits that summer brings."

SUBMITTED BY JACQUI PEACH, MEMBER OF STAFF AT LANGSIDE SCHOOL, PART OF DIVERSE ABILITIES PLUS

- 180g plain flour
- 150g soft brown sugar
- 2 teaspoons baking powder
- 65ml sunflower oil
- 1 egg
- 1 teaspoon vanilla essence
- 65ml semi skimmed milk
- 110g fresh raspberries
- 60g blueberries
- 50g white chocolate chips
- A little demerara sugar to sprinkle on the top

1. Preheat the oven to 200°C/gas 6.

2. Put the flour, sugar and baking powder in a bowl, mix well and set aside.

3. In a separate bowl, put the oil, egg, vanilla essence, milk and whisk.

4. Add the dry ingredients and stir until fully incorporated.

5. Gently fold in the berries and chocolate chips.

6. Spoon into muffin cases and sprinkle with demerara sugar.

7. Cook for 25 minutes or until golden brown.

Victoria Sandwich

"A classic afternoon treat."

- 175g butter
- 175g caster sugar
- 175g self raising flour
- 3 eggs
- Strawberry jam

Butter cream:
- 175g icing sugar
- 75g butter
- Vanilla extract
- A drop of milk

Submitted by The Rural Farm Shop Co

1. Preheat the oven to 180°C/gas 4.

2. Grease and shake flour around two 7" sandwich tins.

3. Cream together the butter and sugar until light and fluffy.

4. Add the eggs, beating in gradually to the sugar and butter.

5. Sift in the flour, folding in gently.

6. Cook for 25 minutes until the top feels springy when pressed with fingertips.

7. Leave in tins for 5 minutes then turn out onto a wire cooling rack.

8. To make the butter cream, place icing sugar and butter into a bowl and cream until light and fluffy. Add the vanilla extract and a drop of milk, mix well.

9. To assemble, spread strawberry jam over one of the sponge cakes, top with the butter cream, spreading it out evenly.

10. Place the remaining sponge cake on the top and dust with icing sugar.

"BRING BACK HAPPY MEMORIES OF STICKY FINGERS AND LICKING THE SPOON!"

Cooking with kids

CAKE POPS

"This recipe always creates a talking point at any party, enjoyed by children and adults alike, easily tailored to a party theme by choosing different coloured candy melts."

Cake:
- 200g self raising flour
- 225g margarine
- 225g caster sugar
- 25g cocoa powder
- 4 eggs

Frosting:
- 170g soft cheese
- 260g icing sugar
- 3 level tablespoons of butter
- 25g cocoa powder
- 1 tablespoon of milk
- 2 packets of candy melts
- Decorations
- Lollipop sticks

SUBMITTED BY SADIE SMITH, WHOSE SON USES SEVERAL OF THE DIVERSE ABILITIES PLUS SERVICES

1. Preheat the oven to 180°C/gas 4.

2. Grease and line a rectangular tin.

3. Cream together the margarine and sugar until pale and fluffy.

4. Add the beaten eggs, a little at a time, continue to beat the mix.

5. Sift the flour and cocoa powder into the mixture and fold in gently until fully incorporated.

6. Pour into tin and cook for 20 – 25 minutes. Remove and cool on a wire rack.

7. To make the frosting beat the soft cheese, icing sugar, butter and milk together, if too runny add a little more icing sugar.

8. When cool, crumble the cake into a large bowl.

9. Mix with the frosting until it comes together to form a solid lump.

10. Roll the mixture between your hands into walnut sized balls.

11. Place on a piece of baking paper and place in the fridge to chill.

12. Put a stick in the centre of the ball.

13. Melt the candy melts in a bowl over a pan of simmering water.

14. Dip the chilled cake ball into the candy melts, and then decorate by dipping into sugar strands or placing other decorations on the cake pop.

15. Stand sticks in a piece of polystyrene or florist oasis and put back in the fridge until set.

16. Once set they go very hard and can be laid down in a container or left standing upright.

TOP TIP

If the stick pushes through the cake ball before decorating, it is because they need to chill for a bit longer, you can place them in the freezer for 20 minutes.

CHOCOLATE CHIP COOKIES

"A cuddle in a cookie! – These are the cookies my mum bakes when we've had a tough day at school or we're not feeling well and need some cheering up."

- 110g softened butter
- 75g soft brown sugar
- 75g caster sugar
- 1 egg
- ½ teaspoon baking powder
- ½ teaspoon vanilla essence
- 225g plain flour
- 150g chocolate chips

1. Preheat the oven to 180°C/gas 4.

2. Beat together the butter and sugars until creamy.

3. Break an egg into a separate bowl and add the baking powder and vanilla, beat until smooth.

4. Add this to the butter mixture and mix well.

5. Stir in the flour until it's fully incorporated.

6. Add the chocolate chips and mix well.

7. Put teaspoons of mixture onto a greased baking tray, leaving room between each one as they will spread during cooking.

8. Bake for 15 minutes until golden for a soft chewy cookie or 20 minutes for a crispier cookie.

9. Leave to cool on the tray for 5 minutes then place on a wire rack.

SUBMITTED BY GABRIELLE & JAKE SMITH AGED 5 AND 15.

MY FAVOURITE SMOOTHIE

"A fantastic sweet smoothie that I personally love and is really good for you too. It's thick, creamy and tastes out of this world!!"

- 1 banana
- 1 avocado
- 6-8 dates (ensure you take out the tiny stone)
- 1 pint milk or soya milk
- 1 tablespoon honey
- A handful of ice

1. Peel, chop and prepare the banana, avocado and dates.

2. Put all ingredients in a blender.

3. Blend it all up and serve.

SUBMITTED BY DUNCAN JAMES, CELEBRITY TV PRESENTER, WEST END STAR AND SINGER.

CHOCOLATE & CARAMEL CRISPIE CAKES

"This is a really fun and simple recipe. I enjoy making it with my godchildren."

SUBMITTED BY THOMAS MORTIMER, A VOLUNTEER WITH DIVERSE ABILITIES PLUS' SCHOOL HOLIDAY PROJECT CALLED PROJECT MY TIME

- 6 standard size Mars bars (or similar chocolate bar)
- 3 tablespoons golden syrup
- 100g butter
- 150g rice crispies
- 150g milk chocolate

1. Chop the Mars bars into small slices.
2. Place them in a heatproof bowl over a pan of simmering water.
3. Add butter, stir well.
4. Once fully melted, stir in the Golden Syrup.
5. Then fold in the rice crispies.
6. Grease and line a shallow tin with baking paper.
7. Pour the mix into the tin and push down with a wooden spoon.
8. Melt the chocolate in a heatproof bowl over a pan of simmering water.
9. Pour over the crispie base and chill.
10. Cut into squares.

FLAPJACK

"I love this recipe because it's crunchy, chewy, crispy and yummy."

- 175 butter
- 175g oats
- 75g brown sugar
- 2 large heaped tablespoons Golden Syrup
- 25g Coco Pops

1. Preheat the oven to 140°C/gas 1.

2. In a saucepan melt the butter, sugar and syrup.

3. Remove from heat and stir in the oats and Coco Pops.

4. Press into a greased square tin.

5. Cook for 30 – 40 minutes until golden.

6. Cool slightly then cut into slices.

SUBMITTED BY GEORGIA BLAINEY AGED 11. SIBLING OF A CHILD WHO ATTENDS LANGSIDE SCHOOL & SMITHERS

Top Tip

Stir in raisins or chopped dried apricots for a fruity taste.

GINGERBREAD MEN

Recipe submitted by Tasty Marketing

"Our mascot is a gingerbread man and we think this is the perfect recipe! This recipe book is a great opportunity to support a local charity who provide an essential service to people of all ages in the community. Combining a fabulous charity with a love of food is definitely a perfect recipe!"

- 320g plain flour
- 100g butter
- 100g dark muscovado sugar
- 4 tablespoons Golden Syrup
- 4 teaspoons ground ginger
- 1 teaspoon bicarbonate of soda

1. Preheat the oven to 170°C/gas 3.

2. Combine the flour, ginger and bicarbonate of soda in a bowl and mix well. Put to one side.

3. Put the butter, sugar and syrup in a pan and melt over a gently heat. Stir until it has completely melted but do not let it boil.

4. Pour this into the dry ingredients, using a wooden spoon mix together until it forms a dough.

5. Sprinkle your worktop with a little flour and place the ball on it for rolling,

6. Roll this until it is about 5mm in thickness, cut out your shapes using a gingerbread man cutter.

7. Place them on a greased baking tray.

8. Cook for 10 minutes.

9. Cool on a wire rack.

10. Once cool decorate with icing, chocolate or anything of your choice.

ICED BISCUITS

"I made these biscuits at school during a technology lesson, and now we use it a lot at home, especially to make biscuits for presents or at Christmas."

SUBMITTED BY JAKE SMITH AGE 15
JAKE'S TWIN BROTHER ATTENDS LANGSIDE
SCHOOL & SMITHERS

- 175g plain flour
- 110g soft butter
- 75g sugar
- 1 level teaspoon mixed spice

Icing:
- 225g icing sugar
- Decorations

1. Preheat oven to 180°C/gas 4

2. Place the flour, sugar and butter in a bowl, mix and knead until a dough is formed.

3. Roll out about 5mm thick and using shaped cutters stamp out the required biscuit shape.

4. Place on a lightly greased tray.

5. Cook for 8 – 10 minutes, when cooked remove and cool on a wire rack.

6. Once cool, add water to icing sugar, a few drops at a time.

7. Add a few drops of chosen colour.

8. Spread over the biscuits and decorate.

Mud pie cake

"This recipe was submitted by Noah as a mud pie using soil, worms & slugs. It made us all laugh so much we just had to turn it into a cake."

Submitted by Noah Taylor aged 2
Noah's Dad works for Diverse
Abilities Plus

- 175g margarine
- 175g caster sugar
- 150g self raising flour
- 3 eggs
- 25g cocoa powder

Icing:
- 225g icing sugar
- 110g butter
- 25g cocoa powder
- 2 tablespoons milk

Decoration:
- 4 chopped flake bars
- Jelly worms

1. Preheat the oven to 180°C/gas 4.

2. Cream together the margarine and sugar, until pale and fluffy.

3. Add the beaten eggs a little at a time. Beat well.

4. Sift the flour and cocoa powder into the bowl and gently fold in until it is fully incorporated.

5. Grease and shake flour around a tin (any shape is fine).

6. Pour the mixture into the tin and cook for approx 20 minutes until the middle feels springy when gently pressed with fingertips.

7. Cool in the tin for a few minutes then turn out onto a wire cooling rack.

8. To make the icing, beat all the icing ingredients together until well mixed and creamy, (add a little more milk if icing is too stiff).

9. Spread the icing on the top of the cake, on this occasion presentation is not important, and pile with chopped flakes and place worms around the cake.

PANCAKES WITH A MIXED BERRY SALSA

"How often do your children ask to do some cooking, only to find you haven't got the right ingredients in? Well our pancake recipe uses store cupboard basics, so no need for that quick dash to the shops."

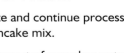

SUBMITTED BY THE WHITE PEPPER & DIVERSE ABILITIES PLUS BAKING TEAM

Pancakes:

- 225g plain flour
- 3 teaspoons of baking powder
- 2 teaspoons of vegetable oil
- 375ml milk
- 2 eggs

Mixed berry salsa and coulis:

- Strawberries
- Raspberries
- Blueberries
- 2 tablespoons icing sugar
- Alternatively a packet of mixed frozen berries

Top Tip

If you do not have berries at hand, simply use both lemon juice and sugar or drizzle melted chocolate over the pancakes.

1. Place the flour, baking powder, vegetable oil, milk and eggs in a bowl and beat until smooth and of a thick consistency.

2. Place in the fridge for 30 minutes to rest.

3. Meanwhile, chop all the berries into small pieces and place in a bowl.

4. To make the coulis, take some of the chopped berries and mix with the icing sugar, using a hand blender, whizz until fully pureed.

5. Pass through a sieve into a small saucepan, boil until coulis thickens.

6. To cook the pancakes, heat up the frying pan and add a small drop of oil, then pour a ladle of pancake mix into the middle of the pan.

7. When bubbles start to appear in the middle of the pancake flip it over and cook for 1 minute.

8. Put cooked pancake on a plate and continue process until you have used all the pancake mix.

9. To assemble, place desired amount of pancakes onto a plate, put a spoon of salsa to the side of the pancakes then drizzle the coulis over the top.

PINEAPPLE & CHOCOLATE CHIP MUFFINS

"If there was such a thing as a healthy cake this muffin would be it, using wholemeal flour and hidden fruit (perfect for fussy kids)"

Submitted by Michelle Connor Diverse Abilities Plus Volunteer

- 110g wholemeal flour
- 110g self raising flour
- 1 heaped teaspoon baking powder
- ¾ teaspoon bicarbonate of soda
- ½ teaspoon ground cinnamon
- ½ teaspoon ground ginger
- 175ml vegetable oil
- 75g caster sugar
- 2 eggs
- 225g pineapple chunks
- 110g milk chocolate chips

1. Preheat the oven to 180°C/gas 4.

2. Place the flours into a bowl with the baking powder, bicarbonate of soda, cinnamon and ginger. Mix well.

3. Beat the oil, sugar and eggs together until well blended.

4. Whizz up the drained pineapple chunks with a hand blender until it is a smooth puree.

5. Pour into the egg and oil mixture, mix well.

6. Pour the wet ingredients into the flour, mix thoroughly until all the ingredients are combined, it will be lumpy but that is normal.

7. Stir in the chocolate chips.

8. Pour batter into muffin cases and cook for 25 minutes or until a golden colour.

9. Cool on a wire rack.

Top Tip

These freeze really well, so bake a large batch and always have a snack at hand for hungry children.

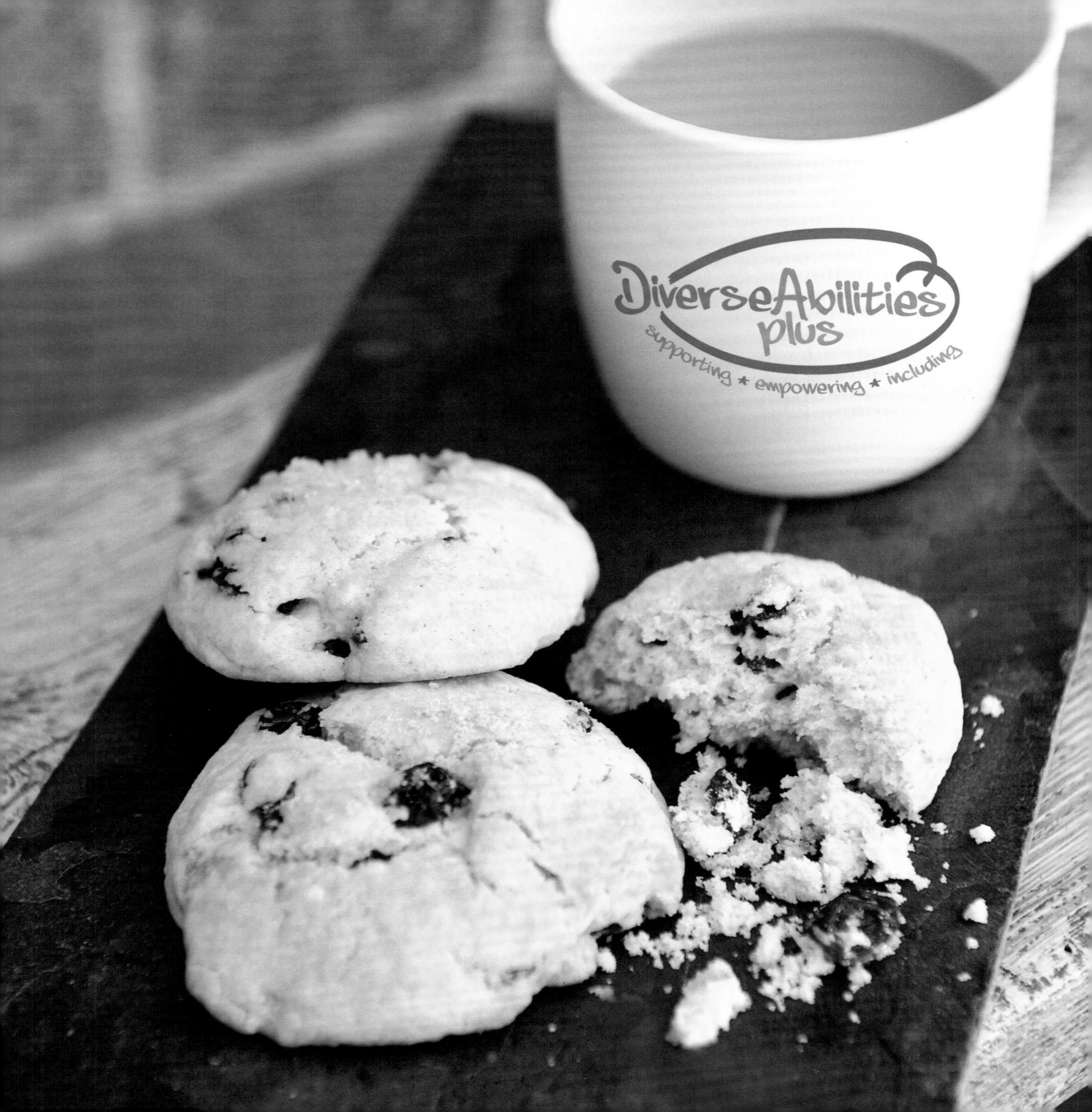
DiverseAbilities plus
supporting * empowering * including

THE SHOW ME SHOW ME COMBO

"A very smoky Earl Grey tea that rocks – in fact rock cakes are the perfect accompaniment."

ROCK CAKES

SUBMITTED BY CHRIS JARVIS AND THE CHILDREN OF LANGSIDE SCHOOL

- 225g self raising flour
- 1 egg
- 110g margarine
- 75g sugar
- 110g dried fruit (sultanas, currants)
- Demerara sugar to sprinkle on the top

1. Preheat the oven to 200°C/gas 7.

2. Sift the flour into a bowl, add the margarine and rub into crumbs with your fingertips.

3. Add the sugar and fruit, mix well.

4. Make a well in the centre of the mixture and pour in the beaten egg.

5. Stir well, using your hands to bring the mixture together to form a loose dough (add a little milk if necessary).

6. Divide into piles of rock shaped mounds and place on a greased baking tray.

7. Sprinkle a little sugar on the top.

8. Cook for 10 – 15 minutes.

9. Cool on a wire tray.

CHRIS' ROCKING TEA

Brew the perfect cuppa using 1 tea bag of Earl Grey and 1 tea bag of lapsang suchong.

A note from Chris Jarvis...

Some people eat to live, I live to eat. For those who love Earl Grey tea... I'd like to introduce the 'Show Me Show Me Combo' developed by myself and a CBeebies producer. Simply mixing one tea bag of Earl Grey mixed with another tea bag of Lapsang Suchong creates a fabulous drink!

Enjoy!

"HEAVENLY, GOOEY, DELICIOUS AND TRULY SCRUMPTIOUS CHOCOLATE RECIPES"

Chocolate Indulgence

CHOCOHOLICS CAKE

"Chocolate heaven cake, perfect for birthdays, can be easily adapted to use your favourite chocolate bar for decoration."

Cake:
- 350g margarine
- 350g caster sugar
- 7 eggs
- 225g self raising flour
- 110g cocoa powder

Icing:
- 225g butter
- 275g icing sugar
- 110g cocoa powder
- Drop of milk
- Raspberry jam for filling
- Your favourite chocolates and bars for decoration

SUBMITTED BY NICOLA ROPER WHOSE DAUGHTER ATTENDS LANGSIDE SCHOOL

1. Preheat the oven to 170°C/gas 3.

2. Grease then shake flour round two 8" sandwich tins.

3. Cream together margarine and sugar until light and fluffy.

4. Add the eggs, a little at a time and beat well to incorporate lots of air.

5. Sift the flour and cocoa powder into the mixture and fold in until it has fully incorporated into the mixture.

6. Divide between the two tins.

7. Cook for 30 minutes.

8. Turn onto a wire rack until cool.

9. Beat together the butter, icing sugar, cocoa powder and a dash of milk.

10. Spread the buttercream over one of the cakes, and then spread raspberry jam over this.

11. Place 2nd cake on the top.

12. Spread the remaining butter cream over the top and sides and decorate with your favourite chocolates.

CHOCOLATE CARAMEL CHEESECAKE

"A recipe I make with my support worker and I love it."

- 200g digestive biscuits
- 125g butter
- 500g soft cheese
- 100ml double cream

- 100g icing sugar
- 1 tin of caramel
- 2 tablespoons chocolate spread
- 1 bar of milk chocolate

SUBMITTED BY ERIC GARLIC WHO IS A CLIENT OF DIVERSE ABILITIES PLUS' SUPPORTED LIVING SERVICE

1. Grease and line an 8" round tin.

2. Melt the butter and add to crushed digestive biscuits.

3. Push into the tin pressing down firmly.

4. Chill.

5. Beat the soft cheese; add the caramel and chocolate spread and mix well.

6. In a separate bowl whisk the cream and icing sugar until stiff, then fold this into the cheese mixture.

7. Pour onto the biscuit base and chill.

8. Before serving grate chocolate over the cheesecake.

CHOCOLATE & PECAN BROWNIES WITH CRÈME ANGLAISE

"Chocolate brownies are a real favourite and a great way to end a meal. The crème anglaise is a wonderful alternative to cream or ice cream."

RECIPE KINDLY DONATED BY DERMOT O'LEARY, PAUL SHOVLIN & JAMES GINZLER

Brownie:

- 150g dark chocolate
- 150g unsalted butter
- 100g pecans, smashed
- 3 eggs
- 225g soft brown sugar
- 1 vanilla pod, split in half lengthways and the seeds scraped out
- 100g plain flour, sifted

Crème Anglaise:

- 250ml double cream
- 250ml semi-skimmed milk
- 1 vanilla pod, split in half lengthways and the seeds scraped out.
- 6 egg yolks
- 90g caster sugar

1. Preheat the oven to 180°C/gas 4.

2. Place the chocolate and butter in a heatproof bowl and set over a pan of just simmering water. Stir gently until the chocolate has melted.

3. Remove from heat and add the smashed pecans.

4. In another mixing bowl whisk the eggs, sugar and vanilla seeds until smooth then fold in the flour.

5. Fold in the melted chocolate, taking care not to over mix.

6. Pour into a baking tin measuring 23cm x 23cm lined with baking paper.

7. Cook for 20 – 25 minutes.

8. To make the crème anglaise, pour the double cream and milk into a saucepan and add the vanilla pod and seeds. Heat gently, do not let it come to a boil.

9. In a mixing bowl whisk the egg yolks and the caster sugar until light and creamy.

10. Strain the milk and cream.

11. Whisk into the egg yolk and sugar mixture then return to the pan and cook over a low heat, stirring continuously with a rubber spatula until mixture starts to thicken. (It should be the consistency of a light custard.)

12. Remove the baking tray from the oven and allow to cool for a few minutes before turning out onto a cooling rack.

13. Cut into squares and serve with the crème anglaise on the side.

FROM THEIR FISHY FISHY COOK BOOK OUT NOW.

PHOTOGRAPHER: JONATHAN GREGSON

BLACKSTRAP HARRY TART WITH RUM–SOZZLED RAISINS

"This gorgeous dessert tart, with its hint of rich blackstrap molasses blended with dark chocolate, is based on our award-winning 'Blackstrap Harry' chocolate."

Sozzled Raisins:

- 100g large raisins
- Freshly squeezed juice of ½ an orange
- 3 strips of orange zest
- 8 tablespoons dark rum
- 1 tablespoon light, soft brown sugar

Ganache Filling:

- 250g dark chocolate (70% cocoa solids) chopped
- 300ml double cream
- 1 tablespoon blackstrap molasses
- 100g light soft brown sugar
- ½ teaspoon sea salt

Tart Base:

- 200g good quality, all butter shortbread
- 60g unsalted butter, melted
- ½ tablespoon light, soft brown sugar

RECIPE DONATED BY CLAIRE BURNET, AUTHOR OF CHOCOCO CHOCOLATE COOKBOOK PUBLISHED BY RYLAND PETERS & SMALL

1. Grease and line a 20cm loose based cake tin with baking paper.

2. To prepare the sozzled raisins, put them in a small saucepan, with the orange juice, zest and 6 tablespoons of rum. Bring to the boil and set aside to cool, allowing the raisins to plump up.

3. To make the tart base, crush shortbread to a fine crumb. Melt the butter in a saucepan set over a low heat, stir in the biscuit crumbs and brown sugar. Transfer mixture to cake tin, pressing down firmly into the base, place in the fridge to chill.

4. To make the ganache, put chocolate in a heatproof bowl placed over a saucepan of simmering water. Do not allow the base of the bowl to touch the water.

5. Put the cream, molasses, sugar and salt in a heavy based saucepan and place over a medium heat, stirring continuously as it slowly comes to the boil and the sugar is fully dissolved. Pour the hot cream mixture onto the chocolate and stir until the chocolate has melted.

6. Cool for at least 30 minutes. Once the ganache filling is cool, pour onto the chilled tart base, return to the fridge to chill.

7. Just before serving, take raisins out of marinade and set aside. Remove orange zest and add sugar and remaining 2 tablespoons of rum to the marinade.
Boil for a few minutes until thickened and syrupy.

8. To serve, top with the raisins and spoon the syrup. over the top.

Express Chocolate Cake

"A very moist and chocolately cake which is very quick and easy to make, with the addition of a decorated top can easily be used as a celebration cake."

- 185g plain flour
- 2 tablespoons cocoa powder
- 1 level teaspoon bicarbonate of soda
- 1 level teaspoon baking powder
- 150g caster sugar
- 2 tablespoons Golden Syrup
- 2 eggs, lightly beaten
- 275ml corn oil
- 150ml milk

Icing:
- 40g butter
- 25g cocoa powder, sifted
- 110g icing sugar
- 2 teaspoons milk

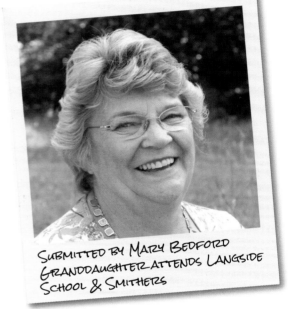

Submitted by Mary Bedford Granddaughter attends Langside School & Smithers

1. Preheat the oven to 170°C/gas 3.

2. Grease and line two 8" sandwich tins.

3. Sift flour, cocoa powder, bicarbonate of soda and baking powder together into a large mixing bowl.

4. Make a well in the centre and add sugar and syrup.

5. Gradually stir in the beaten eggs, oil and milk, beat thoroughly until it becomes a smooth batter.

6. Pour batter into the 2 prepared tins.

7. Cook on the centre shelf for 30 – 40 minutes or until the cakes spring back when lightly pressed with fingertip.

8. Turn onto a wire tray and cool.

9. To make the icing melt the butter in a small pan, stir in the cocoa powder and cook gently for 1 minute.

10. Remove pan from heat and stir in milk and icing sugar. Mix thoroughly.

11. Spread half the icing on one cake and place the other on the top, use the remaining icing to decorate the top.

12. Leave to set.

No cook chocolate cake

SUBMITTED BY SANDRA BLAINEY
PARENT TO CHILD WHO ATTENDS LANGSIDE
SCHOOL AND SMITHERS

"This cake won the **Diverse Abilities Plus** recipe competition. Not surprising as it tastes incredible – chocolatey, crunchy and chewy, what more could you want?"

- 300g plain chocolate
- 75g butter
- 2 tablespoons syrup
- 405g tin of sweetened condensed milk
- 175g dried fruit (apricots, etc)
- 125g sultanas
- 200g rich tea biscuits

1. Break chocolate into pieces and place in a saucepan.
2. Add butter, syrup and condensed milk.
3. Heat gently until the chocolate has melted, stir well.
4. Cut the fruit into small pieces, add this together with the sultanas to the chocolate mix, and stir thoroughly.
5. Crush the biscuits in a bag until you have lots of chunky pieces.
6. Stir into the chocolate mix.
7. Tip the mixture into a loose bottomed cake tin and press down.
8. Chill for 4 hours.
9. Remove from tin and slice.

Nougat Chocolate Mousse

"An indulgent dessert; the perfect way to end a meal."

- 295g Toblerone
- 275ml crème fraîche
- 2 medium egg whites
- 6 tablespoons boiling water

1. Break chocolate into pieces and put in a heatproof bowl along with 6 tablespoons of boiling water.

2. Place over a saucepan of simmering water until fully melted.

3. Allow to cool and thicken.

4. Fold in crème fraîche.

5. Whisk the egg whites to form stiff peaks.

6. Fold egg whites into the chocolate mixture.

7. Pour into individual ramekin dishes.

8. Chill for 6 hours.

RECIPE SUBMITTED BY HELEN ALEXANDER FUNDRAISING MANAGER, DIVERSE ABILITIES PLUS

Top Tip

To serve, sprinkle with sifted cocoa powder and grated chocolate.

TIPSY CHOCOLATE TRIFLE

"This recipe was given to me by a friend, as a dessert you can make when you have no time and with ingredients you keep in the cupboard for an emergency. An easily adapted recipe to suit individual tastes, you can add chocolate muffins, use extra chocolate or fresh cream instead of long life cream."

- 50g dark chocolate
- 1 packet double chocolate chip cookies
- 6 tablespoons of sherry
- 1 small carton of ready made custard

- 284ml long life double cream
- A little grated chocolate for decoration

RECIPE SUBMITTED BY CAROLYN ASHBY
WIFE OF HEAD TEACHER AT LANGSIDE SCHOOL

1. Melt the chocolate in a bowl over a pan of simmering water.

2. Add the sherry and mix well.

3. Add half the custard to the chocolate mix and stir thoroughly.

4. Break the biscuits into small pieces, then add to the chocolate mix, stirring until completely coated.

5. Pour this mixture into the bottom of a trifle dish and chill in the fridge.

6. To make topping, whip the cream until it forms peaks, then slowly whisk in the remaining custard.

7. Spread this over the chilled chocolate base.

8. Grate a little dark chocolate on the top, and return to the fridge to chill.

Top Tip

To make it extra tipsy soak the biscuits in five spoonfuls of sherry.

WARM CHOCOLATE FONDANT

"Everybody's favourite! Warm, dark chocolate sponge with a melting middle."

Sponge:
- 30g unsalted butter
- 150g dark chocolate, chopped
- 2 eggs
- 1 ½ egg whites
- 45g caster sugar

Chocolate centre:
- 75g dark chocolate, chopped
- 5 tablespoons double cream

To serve:

Single scoop of ice cream (frozen & then) rolled in chopped nuts

Submitted by White Pepper Cookery School

1. Preheat oven to 180°C/gas 4.

2. Grease and shake flour or cocoa powder around 4 oven proof pudding basins or dariole moulds.

3. To make the chocolate centre, heat the cream in a saucepan until it begins to boil.

4. Pour onto the chopped chocolate and stir until both are fully incorporated, place in the fridge and allow to set.

5. To make the sponge, gently melt the butter and chocolate in a saucepan, remove from heat and put to one side.

6. Place 3 ½ egg whites into a clean bowl and whisk until stiff.

7. Add the sugar 1 tablespoon at a time, continuing to whisk all the time, the whites should appear stiff and glossy.

8. Enrich the chocolate mixture with the egg yolks and beat briefly to incorporate.

9. Fold the meringue into the chocolate mixture in 3 batches.

10. Remove the chocolate centre from the fridge and roll into 4 small balls (walnut sized).

11. Fill the moulds with half the sponge mixture. Place a chocolate ball on the top. Place the remaining mixture on top and level the top of the moulds.

12. Bake for 12 – 14 minutes or until springy and well risen. The edge of the sponge should also leave the sides of the mould.

Top Tip

Over cooking will result in a solid sponge with no liquid centre, check after 10 minutes. Serve hot with ice cream.

WHITE CHOCOLATE CHEESECAKE

"My friend's favourite, whom I've known for many years. A very indulgent cheesecake."

- 110g digestive biscuits
- 50g butter
- 400g white chocolate
- 284ml double cream
- 250g full fat cream cheese
- 250g mascarpone cheese

Recipe submitted by Jacqui Peach who works at Langside School

1. Place digestive biscuits in a bowl and bash with a rolling pin until it resembles breadcrumbs.

2. Melt the butter and add to the biscuits.

3. Press into a round tin and chill. (Use a loose bottom tin for ease of removal later.)

4. Melt the chocolate in a heatproof bowl over a saucepan of simmering water, once fully melted, set aside to cool slightly.

5. Gently beat the cream cheese and mascarpone cheese together.

6. Whisk the double cream.

7. Fold the cream into the cheese mixture.

8. Stir in the cooled chocolate.

9. Pour onto the biscuit base.

10. Chill for 3 hours or overnight.

11. Serve decorated with red berries.

"REALLY INDULGENT PUDDINGS AND DESSERTS "

Cold Desserts

BLACK CHERRY CHEESECAKE

"This lovely recipe has won me plenty of brownie points with my girlfriend, family and friends. It quite literally puts the cherry on the cheesecake!"

- 200g digestive biscuits
- 125g soft butter
- 300g cream cheese
- 60g icing sugar
- 1 teaspoon vanilla extract
- ½ teaspoon lemon juice
- 250ml double cream
- 1 jar of good quality black cherry conserve (not jam)

Recipe submitted by Hugh Felstead Member of staff at Diverse Abilities Plus

1. Place the digestive biscuits in a bowl and bash with a rolling pin until it resembles breadcrumbs.

2. Melt the butter and add to the biscuits.

3. Press into a 20cm spring form tin and chill.

4. Beat together the cream cheese, icing sugar, vanilla and lemon juice until smooth.

5. In a separate bowl, whip the double cream.

6. Fold the cream into the cheese mixture.

7. Pour onto biscuit base.

8. Chill for 3 hours or overnight.

9. When ready to serve spoon over the black cherry conserve.

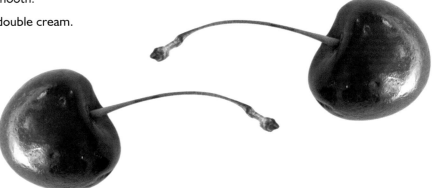

LA FOSSE ELDERFLOWER SUMMER PUDDING

Pudding:
- 100g redcurrants
- 100g blackcurrants
- 350g raspberries
- 350g strawberries
- 150g sugar
- 8 slices of white bread
- 100ml elderflower cordial

Elderflower cordial:
- 20 heads of elderflower
- 1.8kg caster sugar
- 1.2 litres of water
- 2 lemons
- 75g citric acid

SUBMITTED BY LA FOSSE AT CRANBORNE.

1. Mix the fruit and sugar together.

2. Split the mix into two and blitz half until you have a smooth coulis.

3. Add elderflower cordial gradually into the coulis to taste.

4. Cut the crusts off the bread and cut 8 discs of bread from 4 slices to fit the top and bottom of the pudding basins or small moulds. Cut the remaining 4 slices into 3 strips each.

5. Dip the bread into the fruit coulis, leave to soak up the juice.

6. Line the individual pudding basins with cling film, leaving extra around the top sufficient to seal in the puddings.

7. Place soaked bread disc in the bottoms of the basins followed by 2 or 3 strips to form the sides.

8. Generously ladle in the berry mix into the bread lined basins and top with final disc.

9. Twist cling film over the top to compress the puddings, then leave overnight for best results to allow flavours to infuse and the pudding to become structurally sound.

ELDERFLOWER CORDIAL

1. Rinse the flower heads whilst boiling the water.

2. Mix sugar and lemon juice together.

3. Pour the liquid onto the rinsed flowers and leave overnight to infuse.

4. Strain and bottle in clean screw top bottles.

ETON MESS

"This recipe is a colourful and fun dessert for any occasion. The different textures and flavours blend to create a bowl full of creamy goodness every time!"

Meringue:
- 425g caster sugar
- 6 egg whites
- 1 ½ teaspoons lemon juice
- 3 teaspoons icing sugar (sifted)

- 500ml double cream
- 1 punnet of strawberries

Coulis:
- Strawberries
- 1 teaspoon icing sugar

RECIPE SUBMITTED BY DAVE AUSTIN
MEMBER OF STAFF AT DIVERSE ABILITIES PLUS

1. Preheat the oven to 120°C/gas ½ .

2. Place the egg whites, caster sugar and lemon juice in the bowl of an electric mixer and whisk on high speed for exactly 15 minutes.

3. Fold in the sifted icing sugar.

4. Spread onto a baking tray covered with baking paper.

5. Cook for 1 ½ hours. Turn off the oven and leave the meringue in oven to further dry out, ideally overnight but not essential.

6. Whip the cream until it forms soft peaks.

7. Wash, hull and chop the strawberries.

8. To make the coulis, use 2 tablespoons of the chopped strawberries, place in a jug with 1 teaspoon of icing sugar and blitz with a hand blender, pass through a sieve into a small saucepan.

9. Boil the coulis until it thickens, to achieve a really red colour add a couple of drops of red food colouring.

10. To assemble, break the meringue into pieces.

11. In individual glass dishes or wine glasses, layer up the meringue, strawberries, cream and coulis, repeat until its level with the top of the glass bowl.

12. Drizzle the remaining coulis over the top then finish with a strawberry and a sprig of mint.

Top Tip

The meringue can be made a few days in advance and stored in an airtight container.

GOOEY CHOCOLATE BROWNIE ICE CREAM

"I love making this recipe as it's a real winner with family & friends, definitely a recipe to share for all to enjoy.

These brownies make a delicious luxury ice cream, we think this homemade version tastes even better than a certain well known American ice cream brand."

- 175g dark chocolate
- 175g butter
- 350g caster sugar
- 175g self raising flour
- 3 eggs
- 1 litre tub of good quality vanilla ice cream

BROWNIE RECIPE SUBMITTED BY ELEANOR DYBLE. PLAY WORKER FOR COPING WITH CHAOS, PART OF DIVERSE ABILITIES PLUS

1. Preheat the oven to 200°C/gas 6.

2. Grease and line a square baking tin with baking paper.

3. Melt the chocolate and butter in a saucepan over a low heat, stir well.

4. Add the sugar, then the flour a little at a time continually stirring, until it is fully incorporated.

5. Beat the eggs in a separate bowl then stir into the chocolate mixture.

6. Pour into the baking tin.

7. Cook at 200°C/gas 6 for the first 10 minutes and 180°C/gas 4 for a further 20 minutes.

8. Cool in tin slightly, then remove and place on a wire rack.

9. Put ice cream into a bowl to soften.

10. Cut brownie into small cubes.

11. Fold them into the softened ice cream very gently.

12. Place in freezer to use when required.

Top Tip

Use this ice cream to make a chocolate brownie sundae. Reserve a few cubes of brownie to place at the bottom of a glass dish, top with the ice cream and warm chocolate sauce.

Hazelnut Shortbread with Lemon Mascarpone

"Having taught 1000s of adults and children to cook since 2001, I realise how fortunate most people are compared to those that **Diverse Abilities Plus** helps. It is imperative that people are made aware of this fantastic charity and the amount of support they give."

Shortbread:

- 75g plain flour
- 20g ground hazelnuts
- 30g cornflour
- 90g unsalted butter
- 30g icing sugar

Lemon mascarpone:

- 250g mascarpone cheese
- 500ml double cream
- Zest of an unwaxed lemon
- Icing sugar to sweeten

To finish:

- Fresh raspberries

RECIPE SUBMITTED BY JULIA'S KITCHEN

1. Preheat the oven to 180°C/gas 4.

2. Sift the icing sugar into a bowl and add the softened butter, cream well.

3. Sift the two flours into the bowl, add the hazelnuts and bring together to form a dough.

4. Roll into a cylinder, wrap in cling film and rest in the fridge (approx 1 hour).

5. Cut slices of shortbread dough and carefully roll into biscuits using a round cutter.

6. Cook for approx 15 – 20 minutes until lightly browned.

7. To make the lemon cream, place the mascarpone in a large bowl.

8. Add the lemon zest and mix well.

9. Pour in the double cream whisking continuously.

10. Add the icing sugar, testing until correct taste is achieved. Keep whisking until mixture forms soft peaks.

11. To assemble, place a shortbread on a serving plate spread thickly with the cream mixture, place another shortbread on top and repeat this until you have a three shortbread stack, dust the top with icing sugar and fresh raspberries (optional).

LEMON MERINGUE PIE

"A very easy sweet yet sharp lemon tart."

Pastry:
- 150g plain flour
- 75g butter
- 50g caster sugar
- 2 egg yolks

Filling:
- 300g jar of lemon curd
- 1 lemon (zest and juice)
- 1 egg beaten
- 2 tablespoons crème fraîche

Meringue:

3 egg whites

175g sugar

SUBMITTED BY SANDRA BLAINEY
PARENT TO A CHILD WHO ATTENDS LANGSIDE
SCHOOL & SMITHERS

1. Preheat the oven to 170°C/gas 3.

2. Rub together the butter and flour until it resembles fine breadcrumbs.

3. Add the sugar and mix.

4. Make a well in the mixture and pour in egg, mix to form a dough. (You may need to add a little milk.)

5. Roll out and line a greased flan dish. Trim off the excess pastry and prick with a fork.

6. Place in the oven to blind bake for 5 minutes. (Line pastry with baking paper and baking beans or dried rice.)

7. Mix together lemon curd, lemon zest, lemon juice, egg and crème fraîche.

8. Pour into the pastry case.

9. Bake for approx 25 minutes until it appears set.

10. To make the meringue, whisk egg whites until it forms stiff peaks.

11. Gradually whisk in the sugar adding a little at a time, pile onto the tart and bake for 10 – 12 minutes until the meringue is a pale biscuit colour.

Top Tip

To simplify this recipe use a shop bought pastry case and do not top with meringue, serve it as a lemon tart.

MANGO DELIGHT

A tropical, summery dessert from Reham who says: "Diverse Abilities Plus is a fantastic charity that supports many families, children and adults across Dorset. Buying this recipe book is a great way to raise money for the charity so it can continue its important work."

Submitted by Reham Khan
BBC South Today presenter and
Diverse Abilities Plus Ambassador

Cake:
- 225g butter
- 225g caster sugar
- 4 medium sized eggs
- 1 teaspoon vanilla extract
- 225g self raising flour

Topping:
- 50g caster sugar
- 500ml double cream
- 250 ml milk
- 100g mangos purée (or chop and purée in a blender ripe fresh mangos)
- 2 teaspoon gelatine
- Fresh ripe mango slices to decorate

1. Preheat the oven to 180°C/gas mark 4.

2. Grease and line a square 8" tin.

3. Cream the butter and sugar together in a bowl until pale and fluffy.

4. Beat in the eggs, a little at a time, and then stir in the vanilla extract.

5. Fold in the flour using a metal spoon.

6. Pour mixture into the tin and cook for 20 – 25 minutes or until golden brown and the top feels light and springy when pressed with fingertips.

7. Place onto a wire rack to cool.

8. To make the topping, put the cream and milk into a pan.

9. Add the sugar and mango purée.

10. Sprinkle the gelatine over the mixture whisking as you do so.

11. Bring the mixture slowly to the boil, whisking constantly.

12. To assemble, break up the sponge and place in the bottom of a trifle dish or individual glass bowls.

13. Pour some of the mango purée over the sponge, so that it soaks in.

14. Pour the topping over the sponge and place in the fridge to set.

15. To serve decorate with fresh mango slices.

MINT CHOCOLATE CHIP MILLE FEUILLE

"Purbeck Ice Cream is a Dorset producer of exceptional real dairy ice cream and true to our Dorset routes we like to help and support local charities like Diverse Abilities Plus. We hope people enjoy making our Mint Chocolate Chip Mille Feuille Recipe – we certainly do."

SUBMITTED BY PURBECK ICE CREAM

Chocolate discs:
- 400g dark chocolate
- 200g demerara sugar
- Peppermint essence to taste

- 1 tub Purbeck Ice Cream - Mint Choc Baby Chip

Sweet pesto:
- 100g fresh mint
- 25g toasted pine nuts
- 100g sugar
- 100g water
- 1 lemon juice

1. To make the chocolate discs, place the chocolate and the peppermint essence in a bowl set over, but not in, a saucepan of steaming water. Stir occasionally so that the chocolate melts evenly.

2. Allow the mixture to cool, so it is no longer hot to the touch but still fluid.

3. Stir in the sugar; spread the mixture thinly over a large piece of baking paper. Place another piece of parchment over the top and roll with a rolling pin to an even thinness.

4. Refrigerate until set.

5. When the chocolate is firm but not brittle, cut into discs using a fluted cutter.

6. To make the sweet pesto, boil the sugar and water to make a syrup, allow to cool.

7. Put the mint leaves, pine nuts, lemon juice and sugar syrup in a tall container and liquidise.

8. Taste the pesto and correct the taste with fresh lime juice and extra mint.

9. To assemble the dish, cut out discs of Purbeck Mint Choc Baby Chip Ice Cream and layer with the chocolate discs. (Suggest 3 discs of chocolate & 2 of ice cream.)

10. Dust with cocoa powder and drizzle the sweet pesto around the mille feuille.

PROFITEROLES

"I have made this recipe for many years; it is a mouth watering combination of choux pastry, cool cream and a rich hot chocolate sauce."

- 150ml water
- 50g butter
- 75g plain flour
- Pinch of salt
- 2 eggs, beaten

- 300ml whipping cream
- 110g plain chocolate
- 75g butter
- 3 tablespoons Golden Syrup

SUBMITTED BY SANDRA BLAINEY
PARENT OF ELIZABETH WHO ATTENDS
LANGSIDE SCHOOL & SMITHERS

1. Preheat the oven to 220°C/gas 7.

2. Heat the water and butter in a pan until butter has melted, then bring to a rapid boil.

3. Remove from heat and quickly stir in flour and salt.

4. Allow to cool slightly.

5. Then gradually beat in the eggs a little at a time.

6. Spoon a walnut sized amount onto a baking tray covered with baking paper.

7. Cook for 20 – 25 minutes until golden and crisp.

8. Cool on a wire rack.

9. Whip the cream, spoon into a piping bag, make a small slit in the side of the choux pastry to allow you to put the piping bag nozzle in and fill with cream.

10. Pile filled pastries onto a serving plate.

11. Melt the chocolate, butter and syrup gently together.

12. Pour over the profiteroles and serve.

Top Tip

Flick a bit of water over the choux buns before cooking, which creates steam which helps to dry them out.

STRAWBERRY & CHOCOLATE PAVLOVA

**"The easiest meringue ever!!!
Yet such an impressive dessert."**

- 6 egg whites
- 425g caster sugar
- 1 ½ teaspoons lemon juice
- 3 teaspoons icing sugar

- 2 pots of double cream
- Large punnet of strawberries
- Large bar of Dairy Milk chocolate

1. Preheat oven to 120°C/gas ½.

2. Place all the meringue ingredients in the bowl of an electric mixer and whisk on high speed for 15 minutes.

3. Spread over a tray covered with baking paper, shape it into a large circle and ensure that the edges are higher than the middle.

4. Cook for 1 – 1 ½ hours, it can be left in a turned off oven to dry out further after cooking time is finished (overnight is fine but not essential).

5. Wash strawberries and dry thoroughly.

6. Break chocolate into pieces and put in a heatproof bowl, place over a saucepan of simmering water until melted.

7. Dip each strawberry into the chocolate about half way and place on a plate covered in baking paper, chill until the chocolate has hardened.

RECIPE SUBMITTED BY ASHLEY WEEDON COMMUNITY FUNDRAISER AT DIVERSE ABILITIES PLUS

8. Whip the cream until it forms soft peaks.

9. Spread the cream over the meringue base.

10. Top with strawberries.

Top Tip

If time is of the essence, simply pile with halved strawberries and grate chocolate over the top.

“ FAVOURITE FAMILY CAKES &
BAKES TO CHEER UP A DULL DAY ”

Comfort Cooking

Apple & Blackberry Pie

"This pie is a firm favourite amongst the adults who use the Barnabas service."

Pastry:
- 225g plain flour
- 110g margarine
- 25g caster sugar
- 1 egg yolk (reserve white for glazing the lid of pie)

Filling:
- 4 large cooking apples
- 50g blackberries
- 25g brown sugar
- 75g caster sugar
- ½ teaspoon cinnamon

Submitted by Chris Collins
Cook at Barnabas Adult Day
Opportunities Centre

1. Preheat oven to 180°C/gas 4.

2. To make the pastry, place the flour, margarine and sugar in a bowl, mix and rub into fine breadcrumbs.

3. Add the egg yolk and enough cold water to form a dough.

4. Divide the dough into 2 lumps, one slightly bigger than the other.

5. Roll out the larger lump until ½ cm thick, and then carefully place it into an 8" round pie dish. Push down the edges carefully and let the pastry overhang the top slightly, trim off any excess.

6. To make the filling, peel and dice the apple.

7. Place in a saucepan with a little water and cook for approx 3 minutes.

8. Add the blackberries, cinnamon and sugar, but do not place it back on the heat.

9. Fill the pastry with the fruit mixture.

10. Take the remaining lump of pastry and roll out to the same thickness as before.

11. Brush egg white around the top of the pastry already in the pie dish and then place the rolled out pastry over the top of the pie, trim and pinch together the pastry rim.

12. Brush the top with egg white and sprinkle with sugar.

13. Use any scraps of left over pastry to make leaves and place on top of the pie for decoration.

14. Cook for 20 minutes or until golden.

BABAS WITH RUM SYRUP, PISTACHIOS & CREAM

"A French pastry steeped in history and rum! Made by making enriched pastry dough and cooked thoroughly to create a dry porous sponge texture."

Pastry dough:

- 5g salt
- 10g fresh yeast or 1 teaspoon dried yeast
- 2 eggs, beaten
- 200g bread flour
- 15g sugar
- 100ml warm water
- 50g butter

Rum syrup:

- 150ml water
- 150g sugar
- 75ml dark rum
- 1 vanilla pod, seeds removed or 1 teaspoon vanilla extract

To finish:

- Spare rum syrup
- 50 – 75g pistachios, finely chopped
- Double cream, whipped (optional)
- Raw fresh fruit, strawberries, raspberries, blackberries, grapes (optional)

SUBMITTED BY WHITE PEPPER COOKERY SCHOOL

1. Preheat the oven to 190°C/gas 5, 30 minutes into the recipe.

2. Butter the moulds.

3. Sift the flour and salt into a bowl.

4. Dissolve the sugar and yeast in a little of the warm water or as directed by the instructions on the packet.

5. Beat the egg with the water and add in a steady stream to the flour, mixing all the time (with your hands as a paddle). The dough should become elastic.

6. Continue to work the dough to produce a dough that is elastic but quite liquid.

7. Add the butter either with your hand or wooden spoon, continue to beat until fully incorporated.

8. Cover the dough and leave to rise in a warm place for 25 minutes (25°C).

9. Knock the air from the risen dough (carbon dioxide) and fill each mould half full.

10. Allow to double in size in a warm place (35°C).

11. Bake the pastries for approx 22 minutes until light, dry and golden brown, cool on wire racks.

12. To make the rum syrup, dissolve the sugar in the water and bring to the boil. Boil until it turns syrupy. Add the rum and vanilla and boil for a further minute or two.

13. While the pastries are still warm use a skewer to make holes in each of the sponges. Carefully pour on the syrup, allowing the sponges to soak it all up.

14. Allow to cool before glazing with spare rum syrup and decorating with pistachios and cream.

BANANA & WALNUT BREAD

"A really easy recipe that works every time and whilst simple always impresses. It's lovely eaten hot as a pudding with custard or cold with a cup of tea."

- 200g plain flour
- 2 teaspoons of baking powder
- Pinch of salt
- 65g butter
- 115g caster sugar
- 3 ripe bananas
- 2 eggs, beaten
- 50g walnuts
- I teaspoon vanilla extract
- Demerara sugar to sprinkle on the top

SUBMITTED BY CHARLOTTE CURTIS HEAD OF BUSINESS RESOURCES AT DIVERSE ABILITIES PLUS

1. Preheat the oven to 180°C/gas 4.
2. Grease a loaf tin.
3. Put the flour, baking powder and salt into a bowl and mix.
4. In a separate bowl, cream together the butter and sugar until light and fluffy.
5. Mash the bananas and add to the butter mix.
6. Beat in the eggs a little at a time.
7. Add the dry ingredients, mix well until fully incorporated.
8. Add the walnuts and vanilla extract, mix well.
9. Spoon into the loaf tin and sprinkle with demerara sugar.
10. Cook for 50 – 60 minutes, leave to cool in the tin.

GRANDAD'S FAVOURITE DORSET APPLE CAKE

"I always make this when my dad visits, as it's his favourite."

- 110g butter
- 175g soft brown sugar
- 225g self raising flour
- 2 eggs
- 2 large Bramley apples
- 1 teaspoon of lemon juice
- 50g sultanas

1. Preheat the oven to 180°C/gas 4.
2. Grease and line a loaf tin with baking paper.
3. Peel and chop the apple into chunks.
4. Sift the flour into a bowl and rub in the butter.
5. Stir in the sugar, chopped apple and sultanas.
6. Stir in the beaten eggs and juice to make a dryish mixture.
7. Press into the tin.
8. Cook for 30 – 40 minutes until firm and golden brown.
9. Leave to cool in the tin before turning out.

RECIPE SUBMITTED BY SANDRA BLAINEY
SANDRA'S DAUGHTER ELIZABETH IS A PUPIL
AT LANGSIDE SCHOOL

Top Tip

Serve cold or warm with a scoop of vanilla ice cream.

Dream cake

"Mum used to make this cake as a special treat and it reminds me of the start of summer holidays, picnics and on occasions, coming home from school and managing to get a piece before tea!!"

Base:
- 110g butter
- 225g self raising flour
- 50g brown sugar

Topping:
- 2 eggs
- 175g caster sugar
- 25g ground rice
- 50g chopped cherries
- 75g chopped walnuts
- 25g desiccated coconut
- ½ teaspoon almond essence

Recipe submitted by Nick Bold, head of Adult Services at Diverse Abilities Plus

1. Preheat the oven to 180°C/gas 4.
2. Place the butter, flour and brown sugar in a bowl and rub in together.
3. Spread into a 8" square tin.
4. Cook for 15 minutes, remove and cool.
5. Whisk the eggs and sugar to a very thick consistency.
6. Stir in the ground rice, cherries, walnuts, coconut and almond essence.
7. Spread evenly over the cooled base.
8. Cook for 20 minutes, do not overcook.
9. Allow to cool and slice into squares.

Top Tip

Replace cherries with dried apricots and other fruit.

LUSCIOUS LEMON CAKE

"This recipe was given to me by an elderly lady who lived next to us when I was growing up. I later looked after her and her husband."

SUBMITTED BY JULIE BALL
SUPPORT WORKER AT DIVERSE ABILITIES PLUS

Cake:
- 2 large eggs
- 110g margarine
- 165g self raising flour
- 165g caster sugar
- 4 tablespoons milk
- Grated rind of 1 lemon

Topping:
- 3 tablespoons of icing sugar
- Juice of 1 lemon

1. Preheat the oven to 180°C/gas 4.
2. Grease and line a loaf tin with baking paper.
3. Place all cake ingredients into a large bowl and beat well until smooth.
4. Pour into the prepared tin.
5. Cook for 50 minutes until the top is springy when pressed with fingertips.
6. Leave to cool in the tin for 10 minutes then place on a wire rack.
7. Gently heat the icing sugar and lemon juice until completely dissolved and becomes like syrup.
8. Prick the top of the cake with a fork.
9. Pour lemon syrup over the cake and leave to cool.
10. Once cool dust with icing sugar.

NANNY'S STICKY TOFFEE PUDDING

"The perfect pud for a large family gathering."

Cake:
- 350g chopped dates
- 110g butter
- 350g sugar
- 350g self raising flour
- 4 eggs
- 2 teaspoons bicarbonate of soda
- 2 teaspoons vanilla essence
- 570ml water

Sauce:
- 225g dark soft brown sugar
- 570ml double cream
- 1 dessert spoon black treacle

RECIPE SUBMITTED BY SANDRA BLAINEY PARENT OF CHILD WHO ATTENDS LANGSIDE SCHOOL & USES THE SMITHERS SERVICE

1. Preheat the oven to 150°C/gas 2.

2. Grease a deep roasting tin.

3. Place the dates in a saucepan with 570ml water and simmer until soft.

4. Cream together butter and sugar until pale and fluffy.

5. Add the eggs and vanilla essence.

6. Beat in the flour until fully incorporated.

7. Add the bicarbonate of soda to the dates (this will fizz).

8. Pour the date mix into the cake mix and stir well.

9. Pour the mixture into the prepared tin.

10. Cook for 25 minutes.

11. For the sauce, simmer the cream, brown sugar and black treacle in a saucepan until it thickens.

12. Pour half of the sauce over the cake and bake for a further 8 minutes.

13. To serve, pour the remaining sauce indulgently over the pudding.

NECTARINE & AMARETTO PASTRIES

"This pastry is delicious served with mascarpone cream and amaretti biscuits."

- 1 packet of puff pastry
- 4 firm but ripe nectarines
- 4 knobs butter
- 4 teaspoons caster sugar
- 12 tablespoons amaretto liqueur

To serve:

- 4 tablespoons mascarpone cheese
- 12 tablespoons double cream
- 8 amoretti biscuits

RECIPE SUBMITTED BY MARK POWELL
CEO OF DIVERSE ABILITIES PLUS AND KEEN COOK

1. Preheat the oven to 200°C/gas 6.

2. Cut the nectarines in half and remove the stone, then cut each half into 4 segments.

3. Place the nectarine pieces on a baking tray and sprinkle with the caster sugar. Place the knobs of butter between the nectarine pieces.

4. Cook for 5 minutes until they have softened.

5. Roll out the puff pastry and cut into four inch squares.

6. Place 4 pieces of nectarine on each puff pastry square.

7. Place the remaining nectarine on another baking tray and pour over the amaretto liqueur.

8. Place both trays in the oven until the pastry is golden brown (between 5 – 10 minutes).

9. Mix the mascarpone and double cream together.

10. Place the pastry on a plate and top with the nectarines cooked in amaretto, spooning any juices over the top.

11. Top with crumbled amoretti biscuits.

12. Serve with a generous helping of the mascarpone cream.

Top Tip

For an alternative serving suggestion, keep the nectarines in half rather than slice them.

RASPBERRY TRAYBAKE

SUBMITTED BY TOM AND KATE
AT SANDBANKS CEREAL

"We love this recipe because it not only tastes great but also is a healthy treat. We hope that you and your family enjoy it as much as we do.

We love to support Diverse Abilities Plus because having a background in physiotherapy we both have a great awareness of the importance of supporting people with both physical and learning disabilities. We know that the care they need is ongoing and is crucial for their health and quality of life. Diverse Abilities Plus is doing a fantastic job at supporting individuals and families across the county for their whole life."

- 150g fresh raspberries
- 50g butter
- 75g clear honey
- 100g Sandbanks Cereal Muesli (seeded batch)
- 100g rolled oats
- 50g ground almonds
- Pinch of salt

1. Preheat oven to 200°C/gas 7.

2. Grease a 20cm x 20cm baking tray.

3. Mash the raspberries roughly and set aside in a bowl.

4. In a medium saucepan, melt the butter and honey with a pinch of salt.

5. Take off the heat and stir in the Sandbanks Cereal Muesli, oats and ground almonds. Mix until they are coated in the butter and honey mixture.

6. Press half the Sandbanks Cereal Mix in an even layer in the baking tray, spread the mashed raspberries on top, then spoon the remaining Sandbanks Cereal mix on the top. Smooth with the back of a spoon and gently press in to the tin.

7. Cook for 10 – 12 minutes or until golden.

8. Remove from oven and leave to cool before slicing into 16 pieces.

Sticky top pineapple upside down cake

"This is the first pudding I made at the age of 14; it became the pudding I always made to accompany our Sunday Roast. My parents were very relieved when I left home and got married, they would say "just to have another pudding on the menu" which always gives us a laugh."

Upside layer:
- 5 pineapple rings
- 5 glace cherries
- 50g butter
- 70g demerara sugar

Cake:
- 175g sugar
- 175g margarine
- 175g self raising flour
- 3 large eggs
- 1 teaspoon baking powder
- 1 teaspoon vanilla essence

Recipe submitted by Sharon Wells
Events Fundraiser at Diverse Abilities Plus

Upside layer:

1. Preheat the oven to 180°C/gas 4.

2. Line an 8" round cake tin with baking paper.

3. Beat the butter and sugar together until smooth and creamy, spread evenly over the base of the tin.

4. Place the pineapple rings on top of the sugar and butter, placing a cherry on the centre of each ring.

Top Tip

Serve with lashings of creamy custard.

Cake:

1. Sift the flour and baking powder into a bowl.

2. Add margarine, sugar, vanilla essence and eggs, beat with an electric mixer until the mix is of a smooth dropping consistency.

3. Pour over the upside layer.

4. Cook on the centre shelf for 35 minutes.

5. Remove from oven and cool for 10 minutes, turn upside down onto a serving plate, carefully removing baking paper.

How to hold a fundraising
BAKE SALE

Now you've made your amazing cakes you're ready to hold a cake sale. This is a super way to raise lots of money for Diverse Abilities Plus and have great fun at the same time.

Firstly you need to identify a good time and place to hold your sale, such as a fete, family party or through a club you're part of. Then you need to choose which recipes you are going to make to sell.

Why not get your friends and family involved? This will help spread the tasks of baking, telling people about your event and selling cakes on the day. It will make it much more fun too.

To get as many people to support your bake sale as possible you need to promote your event. Tell everyone you know and also let Diverse Abilities Plus know what you are doing. The charity can send you posters which you can put up around schools, libraries, local shops and groups to encourage people to attend your bake sale (although remember to ask permission to put posters up). After the bake sale don't forget to donate the funds raised to Diverse Abilities Plus.

You can send a cheque payable to 'Diverse Abilities Plus' to: Diverse Abilities Plus, Unit C, Acorn Business Park, Ling Road, Poole, Dorset, BH12 4NZ.

You can send Diverse Abilities Plus a photo of your bake sale in action too, either to the above address or by emailing **fundraising@diverseabilitiesplus.org.uk**.

Finally, celebrate and be proud! By raising money you have done an amazing thing for charity.

Thank you!

HOW YOUR MONEY WILL HELP DIVERSE ABILITIES PLUS

£10

You've done a great thing through buying this book as you have contributed £10 which can pay for an adult with disabilities to go sailing.

£15

If you held a bake sale that raised £15 it would be enough to provide a music therapy session for a child at Langside School.

£50

By encouraging five people to buy this recipe book you could help purchase some fantastic sensory toys and equipment for use across Diverse Abilities Plus' services.

£150

If you get together with friends to organise a big bake sale that raises £150 your money could buy a package of speech and language equipment to help a child to communicate!

To find out more about how your money can help Diverse Abilities Plus please visit **www.diverseabilitiesplus.org.uk**

INDEX

GLOSSARY OF TERMS

Bake: To cook in an oven with dry heat. The oven should always be heated for 10 to 15 minutes before baking.

Batter: A mixture of flour, liquid and other ingredients that is thin enough to pour.

Beat: To thoroughly combine ingredients and incorporate air with a rapid, circular motion.

Chill: To chill in the refrigerator until a mixture is cool or a dough is firm.

Combine: To stir together two or more ingredients until mixed.

Cool: To cool to room temperature.

Coulis: A thick sauce made from pureed and strained fruit.

Cream: To beat one or more ingredients, usually margarine or butter, sugar and/or eggs, until the mixture is smooth and fluffy.

Crème Anglais: Often served as an accompaniment to sweet soufflés, fruit desserts and cakes. It is a mixture of egg yolks, sugar and milk and/or cream that is cooked only until the yolks coagulate to thicken the custard.

Dariole moulds: A dariole mould looks like a small metal cup. Its shape is cylindrical with a slight taper to it. Anodised aluminum is often used for dariole moulds as this metal is said to help food lift out easily as well as brown evenly.

Dough: A soft, thick mixture of flour, liquids, fat and other ingredients.

Drizzle: To drip a glaze or icing over food.

Dust: To sprinkle lightly with sugar, flour or cocoa.

Fold in: To gently combine a heavier mixture with a more delicate substance such as beaten egg whites or whipped cream without causing a loss of air.

Grease: To rub fat on the surface of a pan or dish to prevent sticking.

Knead: To fold, push and turn dough or other mixture to produce a smooth, elastic texture.

Mix: To stir together two or more ingredients until they are thoroughly combined.

Preheat: An oven that is heated 10 – 15 minutes before baking.

Purée: Foods that have been blended or sieved to the consistency of a soft creamy paste or thick liquid.

Savarin Mould: A ring shaped mould used for cooking Babas.

Sift: To pass a dry ingredient, such as flour, through a sieve to ensure it is lump free.

Simmer: To maintain the temperature of a liquid at just below boiling.

Softened: Margarine, butter, ice cream or cream cheese that is in a state soft enough for easy blending, but not melted.

Soft peaks: To beat egg whites or whipping cream to the stage where the mixture forms soft, rounded peaks when the beaters are removed.

Stir: To combine ingredients with a spoon or whisk using a circular motion.

Whisk: To beat rapidly with a wire whisk or electric mixer to incorporate air into a mixture in order to lighten and increase the volume of the mixture.

CONVERSION CHARTS

Weights Imperial	Metric
½ oz	10 g
¾ oz	20 g
1 oz	25 g
1½ oz	40 g
2 oz	50 g
2½ oz	60 g
3 oz	75 g
4 oz	110 g
4½ oz	125 g
5 oz	150 g
6 oz	175 g
7 oz	200 g
8 oz	225 g
9 oz	250 g
10 oz	275 g
12 oz	350 g
1 lb	450 g
1 lb 8 oz	700 g
2 lb	900 g
3 lb	1.35 kg

Dimensions Imperial	Metric
⅛ inch	3 mm
¼ inch	5 mm
½ inch	1 cm
¾ inch	2 cm
1 inch	2.5 cm
1¼ inch	3 cm
1½ inch	4 cm
1¾ inch	4.5 cm
2 inch	5 cm
2½ inch	6 cm
3 inch	7.5 cm
3½ inch	9 cm
4 inch	10 cm
5 inch	13 cm
5¼ inch	13.5 cm
6 inch	15 cm
6½ inch	16 cm
7 inch	18 cm
7½ inch	19 cm
8 inch	20 cm
9 inch	23 cm
9½ inch	24 cm
10 inch	25.5 cm
11 inch	28 cm
12 inch	30 cm

Volume Imperial	Metric
2 fl oz	55 ml
3 fl oz	75 ml
5 fl oz (¼ pint)	150 ml
10 fl oz (½ pint)	275 ml
1 pint	570 ml
1¼ pint	725 ml
1¾ pint	1 litre
2 pint	1.2 litre
2½ pint	1.5 litre
4 pint	2.25 litres

Oven Temperatures Gas Mark	°F	°C
1	275°F	140°C
2	300°F	150°C
3	325°F	170°C
4	350°F	180°C
5	375°F	190°C
6	400°F	200°C
7	425°F	220°C
8	450°F	230°C
9	475°F	240°C

Published by Diverse Abilities Plus (Charity no. 282197)

Design and layout EC Design and Marketing

ISBN: 978-0-9570517-0-6

Printed in the United Kingdom